LIGHT ON LIFE'S DIFFICULTIES

JAMES ALLEN

TRUE SIGN
PUBLISHING HOUSE

Published by True Sign Publishing House
Address: SY. No. 21/2 & 21/3, Sonnenahalli,
Krishnarajapural, Bengaluru,
Karnataka - 560049 India
E-mail: truesignbooks@gmail.com
Website: www.truesign.in

Light on life's Difficulties
Author: James Allen

ISBN: 978-93-5462-533-6

First Edition: 2021

Contents

I, Truth, am thy Redeemer, come to Me;
Lay down thy sin and pain and wild unrest;
And I will calm thy spirit's stormy sea,
Pouring the oil of peace upon thy breast:
Friendless and love—lo, I abide with thee.

Defeated and deserted, cast away,
What refuge hast thou? Whither canst thou fly?
Upon my changeless breast thy burdens lay;
I am thy certain refuge, even I:
All things are passing; I alone can stay.

Lo I, the Great Forsaken, am the Friend
Of the forsaken; I, whom man despise,
The Weak, the helpless, and despised defend;
I gladden aching hearts and weeping eyes;
Rest thou in Me, I am thy sorrow's end.

Lover, friends and wealth, pleasure and fame—
These fail and change, and pass into decay;
I blame thee not, nor turn my face away:
In My calm bosom hide thy sin and shame.

Foreword

WHEN A MAN enters a dark room he is not sure of his movements, he cannot see objects around him, or properly locate them, and is liable to hurt himself by coming into sudden contact with them. But let a light be introduced, and immediately all confusion disappears. Every object is seen, and there is no danger of being hurt. To the majority, life is such a dark room, and their frequent hurts—their disappointments, perplexities, sorrows and pains—are caused by sudden contact with principles which they do not see, and are therefore not prepared to deal with. But when the light of wisdom is introduced into the darkened understanding, confusion vanishes, difficulties are dissolved, all things are seen in their true place and proportion, and henceforth the man walks open-eyed and unhurt, in the clear light of wise comprehension.

James Allen

CHAPTER-1

The Light That Leads to Perfect Peace

THIS BOOK IS INTENDED to be a strong and kindly companion, as well as a source of spiritual renewal and inspiration to those who aim at a life well-lived and made strong and serene. It will help its readers to transform themselves into the ideal character they would wish to be, and to make their life here that blessed thing which the majority only hope for in some future life.

Our life is what we make it by our own thoughts and deeds. It is our own state and attitude of mind which determine whether we are happy or unhappy, strong or weak, sinful or holy, foolish or wise. If one is unhappy, that state of mind belongs to himself, and is originated within himself. It is a state which responds to certain outward happenings, but its cause lies within and not in those outward occurrences. If one is weak in will, he has brought himself to, and remains in, that condition by the course of thought and action which he has chosen and is still choosing. If one is sinful, it is because he has committed, and continues to commit, sinful acts. If he is foolish, it is because he himself does foolish things.

A man has no character, no soul, no life apart from his thoughts and deeds. What they are, that he is. As they are modified, so does he change. He is endowed with will, and can modify his character. As the carpenter changes the block of wood into a beautiful piece of furniture, so can the erring and sin-stricken man change himself into a wise and truth-loving being.

Each man is responsible for the thoughts which he thinks and the acts which he does, for his state of mind, and the life which he lives.

No power, no event, no circumstance can compel a man to evil and unhappiness. He himself is his own compeller. He thinks and acts by his own volition. No being, however wise and great—even the Supreme—can make him good and happy. He himself must choose the good, and thereby find the happy.

And because of this—that when a man wishes and wills he can find the Good and the True, and enjoy its bliss and peace—there is eternal gladness in the Courts of Truth, and holy joy among the Perfect Ones.

The Gates of Heaven are forever open, and no one is prevented from entering by any will or power but his own. But no one can enter the Kingdom of Heaven so long as he is enamored of, and chooses, the seductions of hell, so long as he resigns himself to sin and sorrow.

There is a larger, higher, nobler, diviner life than that of sinning and suffering, which is so common—in which, indeed, nearly all are immersed—a life of victory over sin, and triumph over evil; a life wise and happy, kind and tranquil, virtuous and peaceful. This life can be found and lived now, and he who lives it is steadfast in the midst of change; restful among the restless; peaceful, though surrounded by strife.

Should death confront him, he is calm. Though assailed by persecution, he knows no bitterness, and his heart is compassionate and filled with rejoicing. In this supremely beautiful life there is no evil, sin and sorrow are ended, and aching hearts and weeping eyes are no more.

The life of triumph is not for those who are satisfied with any lower conditions. It is for those who thirst for it and are willing to achieve it; who are eager for righteousness as the miser is for gold. It is always at hand, and is offered to all, and blessed are they who accept and embrace it. They will enter the World of Truth; they will find the Perfect Peace.

CHAPTER-2
Light on Facts and Hypotheses

WHEN FREEDOM OF THOUGHT and freedom of expression abound, there is much controversy and much confusion. Yet it is from such controversial confusion that the simple facts of life emerge, attracting us with their eternal uniformity and harmony, and appealing forcibly to us with their invisible simplicity and truth. We are living in an age of freedom and mental conflict. Never were religious sects so numerous. Schools—philosophical, occult, and otherwise—abound, and each is eager for the perpetuation and dominance of its own explanation of the universe. The world is in a condition of mental ferment. Contradiction has reached the point of confusion, so that the earnest seeker for Truth can find no solid rock of refuge in the opposing systems which are presented to him. He is thereby thrown back upon himself, upon those incontrovertible facts of his own being which are ever with him—which are, indeed, himself, his life.

Controversy is ranged around hypotheses, not around facts. Fact is fixed and final; hypothesis is variable and vanishing. In his present stage of development, man is not alive to the beautiful simplicity of facts, nor to the power of satisfaction which is inherent in them. He does not perceive the intrinsic loveliness of truth, but must add something to it. Hence, when fact is named, the question almost invariably arises, "How can you explain the fact?" and then follows a hypothesis which leads to another hypothesis, and so on and on until the fact is altogether lost sight of amid a mass of contradictory suppositions. Thus arise the sects and controversial schools.

The clear perception of one fact will lead to the perception of other facts, but a supposition, while appearing to elucidate a fact, does in reality cover it up. We cannot realize the stately splendor of Truth while playing with the gaudy and attractive toys of pretty hypotheses. Truth is not an opinion, nor can any opinion enlarge or adorn it. Fact and supposition are eternally separate, and the cleverest intellectual jugglery— while it may entertain and deceive even the elect—cannot in the slightest degree alter a fact or affect the nature of things-as-they-are. Because of this, the true teacher abandons the devious path of hypothesis, and deals only with the simple facts of life. He fixes the attention of men and women upon these, instead of increasing confusion and intensifying wordy warfare by foisting another assumption upon a world already lost and bewildered in a maze of hypotheses.

The facts of life are ever before us, and can be understood and known if we but abandon our egotism and the blinding delusions which that egotism creates. Man need not go beyond his own being to find wisdom, and the facts of that being afford a sufficient basis on which to erect a temple of knowledge of such beauty and dimensions that it shall at once emancipate and glorify.

Man is; and as he thinks, so he is. A perception and realization of these two facts alone—of man's being and thinking—lead into a vast avenue of knowledge which cannot stop short of the highest wisdom and perfection. One of the reasons why men do not become wise is that they occupy themselves with interminable speculations about a soul separate from themselves—that is, from their own mind—and so blind themselves to their actual nature and being. The supposition of a separate soul veils the eyes of man so that he does not see himself, does not know his mentality, is unaware of the nature of his thoughts without which he would have no conscious life.

Man's life is actual; his thoughts are actual; his life is actual. To occupy ourselves with the investigation of things that are is the way of wisdom. Man considered as above, beyond, and separate from mind and thought, is speculative and not actual, and to occupy ourselves with the study of things that are not, is the way of folly.

Man cannot be separated from his mind; his life cannot be separated from his thoughts. Mind, thought, and life are as inseparable as light, radiance, and color, and are no more in need of another factor to elucidate them than are light, radiance, and color. The facts are all-sufficient and contain within themselves the groundwork of all knowledge concerning them.

Man as mind is subject to change. He is not something "made" and finally completed, but has within him the capacity for progress. By the universal law of evolution he has become what he is, and is becoming that which he will be. His being is modified by every thought he thinks. Every experience affects his character. Every effort he makes changes his mentality. Herein is the secret of man's degradation, and also of his power and salvation if he but utilize this law of change in the right choice of thought.

To live is to think and act, and to think and act is to change. While man is ignorant of the nature of thought, he continues to change for better and worse; but, being acquainted with the nature of thought, he intelligently accelerates and directs the process of change, and only for the better.

What the sum total of a man's thoughts are, that he is. From this sameness of thought with man there is not the slightest fractional deviation. There is a change as a result with the addition and subtraction of thought, but the mathematical law is an invariable quality.

Seeing that man is mind, that mind is composed of thought, and that thought is subject to change, it follows that deliberately to change the thought is to change the man.

All religions work upon the heart, the thought of man, with the object of directing it into purer and higher channels. Success in this direction, whether partial or complete, is called "salvation"—that is, deliverance from one kind of thought, one condition of mind, by the substitution of another thought, another condition.

It is true that the dispensers of religion today do not know this because of the hypothetical veil which intervenes between the fact and their consciousness. But they do it without knowing it, and the

Great Teachers who founded the various religions, built upon this fact, as their precepts plainly show. The chief things upon which these Teachers lay such stress, and so constantly reiterate—such as the purification of the heart, the thinking of right thoughts, and the doing of good deeds—what are they but calls to a higher, nobler mode of thought-energizing forces urging men and women to make an effort in the choosing of thoughts which shall lift them into realms of greater power, greater good, greater bliss?

Aspiration, meditation, devotion—these are the chief means which men in all ages employ to reach up to higher modes of thought, wider airs of peace, vaster realms of knowledge, for "as he thinketh in his heart, so is he." He is saved from himself—from his own folly and suffering—by creating within new habits of thoughts, by becoming a new thinker, a new man.

Should a man by a supreme effort succeed in thinking as Jesus thought—not by imitation, but by a sudden realization of his indwelling power—he would be as Jesus.

In the Buddhistic records there is an instance of a man, not the possessor of great piety or wisdom, who asked Buddha how one might attain the highest wisdom and enlightenment. Buddha replied, "By ceasing all desire." It is recorded that the man let go of all personal desires and at once realized the highest wisdom and enlightenment.

One of the sayings of Buddha runs, "The only miracle with which the wise man concerns himself is the transformation of a sinner into a saint." Emerson also referred to this transforming power of change of thought when he said: "It is as easy to be great as to be small," which is closely akin to that other great and oft-repeated but little understood saying; "Be ye therefore perfect, even as your Father which is in Heaven is perfect."

And, after all, what is the fundamental difference between a great man and a small one? It is one of thought, of mental attitude. True, it is one of knowledge, but then, knowledge cannot be separated from thought. Every substitution of a better for a worse thought is a transforming agency which marks an important advance in knowledge. Throughout the whole range of human life, from the lowest savage to the highest type of man, thought determines character, condition, knowledge.

The mass of humanity moves slowly along the evolutionary path urged by the blind impulse of its dominant thoughts as they are stimulated and called forth by external things. But the true thinker, the sage, travels swiftly and intelligently along a chosen path of his own. The multitudes, unenlightened concerning their spiritual nature, are the slaves of thought, but the sage is the master of thought. They follow blindly, he chooses intelligently. They obey the impulse of the moment, thinking of their immediate pleasure and happiness; he commands and subdues impulse, resting upon that which is permanently right. They, obeying blind impulse, violate the laws of righteousness; he, conquering impulse, obeys the law of righteousness. The sage stands face to face with the facts of life. He knows the nature of thought. He understands and obeys the law of his being.

But the sorrow-burdened victim of blind impulse can open his mental eyes and see the true nature of things when he wishes to do so. The sage—intelligent, radiant, calm—and the fool—confused, darkened, disturbed—are one in essence, and are divided only by the nature of their thoughts. When the fool turns away from and abandons his foolish thoughts and chooses and adopts wise thoughts, lo! he becomes a sage.

Socrates saw the essential oneness of virtue and knowledge, and so every sage sees. Learning may aid and accompany wisdom, but it does not lead to it. Only the choosing of wise thoughts, and, necessarily, the doing of wise deeds, leads to wisdom. A man may be learned in the schools, but foolish in the school of life. Not the committing of words to memory, but the establishing of oneself in purer thoughts, nobler thinking, leads to the peace-giving revelations of true knowledge.

Folly and wisdom, ignorance and enlightenment, are not merely the result of thought, they are thought itself. Both cause and effect—effort and result—are contained in thought.

All that we are is the result of what we have thought.
It is founded on our thoughts; it is made up of our thoughts.

Man is not a being possessing a soul. He himself is soul. He himself is the thinker and doer, actor and knower. His composite mentality is himself. His spiritual nature is rounded by his sphere of thought. He it is that desires and sorrows, enjoys and suffers, loves and hates. The mind is not the instrument of a metaphysical, superhuman soul. Man is soul; mind is being; mind is man.

Man can find himself. He can see himself as he is. When he is prepared to turn from the illusory and self-created world of hypothesis in which he wanders and to stand face to face with actuality, then will he know himself as he is. Moreover, he can picture himself as he would wish to be, and he can create within him the new thinker, the new man. For every moment is the time of choice—and every hour is destiny.

CHAPTER-3

Light on the Law of Cause and Effect in Human Life

HOW FREQUENTLY PEOPLE associate the word "law" with hardness and cruelty! It seems to embody for them nothing but an inflexible tyranny. This arises partly from their inability to perceive principles apart from persons, and partly from the idea that the office of law is solely to punish. Viewed from such an attitude of mind, the term "law" is hazily regarded as some sort of indefinite personality whose business it is to hunt transgressors and crush them with overwhelming punishments.

Now while law punishes, its primary office is to protect. Even the laws which man makes are framed by him to protect himself from his own baser passions. The law of our country is instituted for the protection of life and property, and it only comes into operation as a punishing factor when it is violated. Offenders against it probably think of it as cruel, and doubtless regard it with terror, but to them that obey it, it is an abiding protector and friend, and can hold for them no terror.

So with the Divine Law which is the stay of the Universe, the heart and life of the Cosmos—it is that which protects and upholds, and it is no less protective in its penalties than in its peaceful blessings. It is, indeed, an eternal protection which is never for one moment withheld, and it shields all beings against themselves by bringing all violations of itself, whether ignorant or willful, through pain to nothingness.

Law cannot be partial. It is an unvarying mode of action, disobeying which, we are hurt; obeying, we are made happy. Neither protection nor supplication can alter it, for if it could be altered or annulled the universe would collapse and chaos would prevail. It is not less kind that we should suffer the penalty of our wrongdoing than that we should enjoy the blessedness of our right-doing. If we could escape the effects of our ignorance and sin, all security would be gone, and there would be no refuge, for we could then be equally doubtful of the result of our wisdom and goodness. Such a scheme would be one of caprice and cruelty, whereas law is a method of justice and kindness.

Indeed, the supreme law is the principle of eternal kindness, faultless in working and infinite in application. It is none other than that;

Eternal Love, forever full, Forever flowing free, of which the Christian sings and the "Boundless Compassion" of Buddhistic precepts and poetry.

The law which punishes us is the law which preserves us. When in their ignorance men would destroy themselves, its everlasting arms are thrown about them in loving, albeit sometimes painful, protection. Every pain we suffer brings us nearer to the knowledge of the Divine Wisdom. Every blessing we enjoy speaks to us of the perfection of the Great Law, and of the fullness of bliss that shall be man's when he has come to his heritage of Divine Knowledge.

We progress by learning, and we learn, up to a certain point, by suffering. When the heart is mellowed by love, the law of love is perceived in all its wonderful kindness. When wisdom is acquired, peace is assured.

We cannot alter the law of things, which is of sublime perfection. But we can alter ourselves so as to comprehend more and more of that perfection and make its grandeur ours. To wish to bring down the perfect to the imperfect is the height of folly, but to strive to bring the imperfect up to the perfect is the height of wisdom. Seers of the Cosmos do not mourn over the scheme of things. They see the universe as the perfect whole, not as an imperfect jumble of parts. The Great Teachers are men and women of abiding joy and heavenly peace.

The blind captive of unholy desire may cry;
Ah! Love: could you and I with him conspire

To grasp this sorry scheme of things entire,
Would we not shatter it to bits, and then
Remold it nearer to the heart's desire?

This is the wish of the carnal nature, the wish to enjoy unlawful pleasures to any extent, and not reap any painful consequences. It is such men who regard the universe as a "sorry scheme of things." They want the universe to bend to their will and desire; want lawlessness, not law. But the wise man bends his will and subjects his desire to the Divine Order, and he sees the universe as the glorious perfection of an infinitude of parts.

Buddha always referred to the moral law of the universe as the Good Law, and indeed it is not rightly perceived if it is thought of as anything but good; for in it there can be no grain of evil, no element of kindness. It is no iron-hearted monster crushing the weak and destroying the ignorant, but a soothing love and brooding compassion shielding the tenderest from harm, and protecting the strongest from a too destructive use of their strength. It destroys all evil, it preserves all good. It enfolds the tiniest seedling in its care, and it destroys the most colossal wrong with a breath. To perceive it is the beatific vision. To know it is the beatific bliss; and they who perceive and know it are at peace. They are glad forevermore.

Such is the law which moves the righteousness,
Which none at last can turn aside or stay;
The heart of it is love; the end of it
Is peace and consummation sweet: obey.

CHAPTER-4

Light on Values— Spiritual and Material

IT IS AN OLD-TIME AXIOM that "everything has its price." Everybody knows this commercially, but how few know it spiritually. Business consists of a mutual interchange of equitable values. The customer gives money and receives goods, and the merchant gives goods and receives money. This method is universal, and is regarded by all as just.

In spiritual things the method is the same, but the form of interchange is different. For material things a material thing is given in exchange. Now these two forms of exchange cannot be transposed; they are of reverse natures, and remain eternally separate. Thus a man may bring money to a shop and ask for food, or clothing, or literature, and he will receive goods to the value of his money. But if he were to take a dollar to a teacher of Truth, and ask to be supplied with a dollar's worth of religion, or righteousness, or wisdom, he would be told that those things cannot be purchased with money, that their spiritual nature excludes them from business transactions.

The wise teacher, however, would also tell him that these spiritual necessities must be purchased. Though money cannot buy them, they have their price, and something must be parted with before they can be received. In a word, instead of offering money he must offer up self, or selfishness. For so much selfishness given up, so much religion, righteousness, and wisdom would be immediately received, without fail, and with perfect equity. For if a man is sure of receiving perishable food and clothing for the money he puts down, how much more surely will he receive the imperishable spiritual sustenance and protection for the selfishness which he lays down! Shall the law operate in the lesser and fail in the greater? Man may fail to observe the law, but the law is infallible.

A man may love his money, but he must part with it before he can receive the material comforts of life. Likewise, a man may love his selfish gratifications, but he must give them up before he can receive the spiritual comforts of religion.

Now when a tradesman gives goods for money, it is not that he may keep the money, but that he may give it in exchange for other goods. The primary function of business is not to enable everybody to hoard up money, but to facilitate the interchange of commodities. The miser is the greatest of all failures, and he may die of starvation and exposure while being a millionaire, because he is a worshipper of the letter of money, and an ignorer of its spirit—the spirit of mutual interchange.

Money is a means, not an end; its exchange is a sign that goods are being justly given and received. Thus commerce, with all its innumerable ramifications of detail, is reducible to one primary principle, namely: Mutual interchange of the material necessities of life.

Now let us follow this principle into the spiritual sphere, and trace there its operation. When a spiritual man gives spiritual things—kindness, sympathy, love—and receives happiness in return, it is not that he may hoard and hug to himself that happiness, but that he may give it to others, and so receive back spiritual things. The primary function of spirituality is not to hoard up personal pleasure, but to render actual the interchange of spiritual blessings.

The most selfish man—he whose chief object is the getting of happiness for himself—is a spiritual miser. His mind may perish of spiritual destitution, though he be surrounded with the objects which he has obtained to pander to his pleasure, because he is worshipping the letter of happiness and is ignoring its spirit—the spirit of unselfish interchange. The object of selfishness is the getting of personal pleasure, or happiness; the object of religion is the defusion of virtue. Thus religion, with all its innumerable creeds, may be resolved into one primary principle, namely: Mutual interchange of spiritual blessings.

What, then, are the spiritual blessings? These are kindness, brotherliness, goodwill, sympathy, forbearance, patience, trustfulness, peacefulness, love unending, and compassion unlimited. These blessings, these necessities for the starving spirit of man, can be obtained, but their price must be paid. Unkindness, uncharitableness, ill will, hardness, ill temper, impatience, suspicion, strife, hatred, and cruelty—all these, along with the happiness, the personal satisfaction, which they give, must be yielded up. These spiritual coins, dead in themselves, must be parted with, and when parted with, there will be immediately received their spiritual counterparts, the living and imperishable blessings to which they are a means and of which they are a sign.

To conclude, when a man gives money to a merchant and receives goods in return, he does not wish to have his money again. He has willingly parted with it forever and is satisfied with the exchange. So when a man gives up unrighteousness in exchange for righteousness, he does not wish to have his selfish pleasures back again. He has given them up forever, and is satisfied and at peace.

Thus also, when one bestows a gift, even though it be a material gift, he does not look for the receiver to send him back its value in money, because it is a spiritual deed and not a business transaction. The material thing thus represents the interchange of spiritual blessings, and its accompanying bliss, the bliss of a gift bestowed and that of a gift received.

"Are not two sparrows sold for a farthing?" Everything in the universe—every object and every thought—is valued. Material things have a material value, spiritual things have a spiritual value, and to confound these values is not wise. To seek to purchase spiritual blessings with money, or material luxuries with virtue, is the way of selfishness and folly. It is to confound barter with religion and to make a religion of barter. Sympathy, kindness, love cannot be bought and sold; they can only be given and received. When a gift is paid for, it ceases to be a gift.

Because everything has a value, that which is freely given is gained with accumulation. He who gives up the lesser happiness of selfishness gains the greater happiness of unselfishness. The universe is just, and its justice is so perfect that he who has once perceived it can no more doubt or be afraid. He can only wonder and be glad.

CHAPTER-5
Light on the Sense of Proportion

IN A NIGHTMARE there is no relation of one thing to another; all things are haphazard, and there is a general confusion and misery. Wise men have likened the self-seeking life to a nightmare. There is a close resemblance between a selfish life, in which the sense of proportion is so far lost that things are only seen as they affect one's own selfish aims, and in which there are feverish excitements and overwhelming troubles and disasters, and that state of troubled sleep known as nightmare.

In a nightmare, too, the controlling will and perceiving intelligence are asleep; and in a selfish life the better nature and spiritual perceptions are locked in profound slumber.

The uncultivated mind lacks the sense of proportion. It does not see the right relation of one natural object to another, and is thereafter dead to the beauty and harmony with which it is surrounded.

And what is this sense of proportion but the faculty of seeing things as they are! It is a faculty which needs cultivating, and its cultivation, when applied to natural objects, embraces the entire intelligence and refines the moral character. It enters, however, into spiritual things as well as things natural, and here is more lacking, and more greatly needed. For to see things as they are in the spiritual sphere is to find no ground for grief, no lodging place for lamentation.

Whence spring all this grief and anxiety, and fear and trouble? Is it not because things are not as men and women wish them to be? Is it not because the multiplicity of desires prevents them from seeing things in their true perspective and right proportion?

When one is overwhelmed with grief, he sees nothing but his loss; its nearness to him blots out the whole view of life. The thing in itself may be small, but to the sufferer it assumes a magnitude which is out of proportion to the surrounding objects of life.

All who have passed the age of thirty can look back over their lives at times when they were perplexed with anxiety, overwhelmed with grief, or even, perhaps, on the verge of despair, over incidents which, seen now in their right proportion, are known to be very small.

If the would-be suicide will today stay his hand and wait, he will at the end of ten years marvel at his folly over so comparatively small a matter.

When the mind is possessed by passion or paralyzed with grief, it has lost the power of judgment. It cannot weigh and consider. It does not perceive the relative values and proportions of the things by which it is disturbed. Awake and acting, it yet moves in a nightmare which holds its faculties in thrall.

The passionate partisan lacks a sense of proportion to such an extent that, to him, his own side or view appears all that is right and good, and his opponent's all that is bad and wrong. To this partiality his reason is chained, so that whatever reason he may bring to bear upon the matter is enlisted in the service of bias, and is not exercised in order to find the just relation which exists between the two sides. He is so convinced that his own party is all right, and the other, equally intelligent party is all wrong, that it is impossible for him to be impartial and just. The only thing he understands as justice is that of getting his own way, or placing some ruling power in the hands of his party.

Just as the sense of proportion in things material puts an end to the spirit of repugnance, so in things spiritual it puts an end to the spirit of strife. The true artist does not see ugliness anywhere; he sees only beauty. That which is loathsome to others fills, to him, its rightful place in nature, and it appears in his picture as a thing of beauty. The true seer does not see evil anywhere; he sees universal good. That which is hateful to others, he sees in its rightful place in the scheme of evolution, and it is held dispassionately in his mind as an object of contemplation.

Men and women worry, and grieve, and fight because they lack this sense of proportion, because they do not see things in their right relations. The objects of their turbulence are not things-in-themselves, but their own opinions about things, selfcreated shadows, the unreal creations of an egoistic nightmare.

The cultivation and development of the ethical sense of proportion converts the heated partisan into a gentle peacemaker, and gives the calm and searching of the prophet to the hitherto blind instrument in the clashing play of selfish forces.

The spiritual sense of proportion gives sanity; it restores the mind to calmness; it bestows impartiality and justice and reveals a universe of faultless harmony.

CHAPTER-6

Light on Adherence to Principle

THE MAN OF TRUTH never departs from the divine principles which he has espoused. He may be threatened with sickness, poverty, pain, loss of friends and position, yea, even with immediate death, yet he does not desert the principles which he knows to be eternally true. To him, there is one thing more grievous, more to be feared and shunned than all the above evils put together, and that is—the desertion of principle. To turn coward in the hour of trial, to deny conscience, to join the rabble of passions, desires, and fears in turning upon, accusing, and crucifying the Eternal Christ of Divine Principle, because, forsooth, that principle has not given him personal health, affluence and ease—this, to the man of Truth, is the evil of evils, the sin of sins.

We cannot escape sickness and death. Though we avoid them for a long time, in the end they will overtake us. But we can avoid wrongdoing, we can avoid fear and cowardice. When we habitually avoid wrongdoing and cast out fear, the evils of life will not subdue us when they overtake us, for we shall have mastered them. Instead of avoiding them for a season we shall have conquered them on their own ground.

There are those that teach that it is right to do wrong when the wrong is to protect another; that it is good, for instance, to tell a lie when its object is the well-being of another—that is, that it is right to desert a principle of truthfulness under severe trial. Such teaching has never emanated from the lips of the Great Teachers. It has not been uttered even by those lesser, yet superbly noble men, the prophets, saints and martyrs, for those divinely illuminated men knew full well that no circumstance can make a wrong a right, and that a lie has no saving and protective power. Wrongdoing is a greater evil than pain, and a lie is more deadly and destructive than death. Jesus rebuked Peter for trying to shield his Master's life by wrongdoing, and no rightminded person would accept life at the expense of the moral character of another when it appeared possible to do so.

All men admire and revere the martyrs, those steadfast men and women who feared wrong, cowardice, and lying, but who did not fear pain and death; those who were steadfast and calm in their adherence to principle even when brought to the utmost extremity of trial. Yea, even when the taunts and jeers of enemies assailed them, and the tears and agonies of loved ones appealed to them, they flinched not nor turned back, knowing that the future good and salvation of the whole world depended upon their firmness in that supreme hour. For this, they stand through all time as monuments of virtue, centers of saving, and uplifting power for all humankind.

But he who lied to save himself, or for the sake of the two or three beings whom he personally loved, is rarely heard of, for in the hour of desertion of principle, his power was gone. If he is heard of, he is not loved for that lie. He is always looked upon as one who fell when the test was applied; as an example of the highest virtue he is rejected by all men in all times.

Had all men believed that an untruth was right under extreme circumstances, we should have had no martyrs and saints, the moral fiber of humanity would have been undermined, and the world left to grope in ever deepening darkness.

The attitude which regards wrongdoing for the sake of others as the right thing to do is based on the tacit assumption that wrong and untruth are inferior evils to unhappiness, pain, and death. But the man of moral insight knows that wrong and untruth are the greater evils, and so he never commits them, even though his own life or the lives of others appear to be at stake.

It is easy for a man in the flowery time of ease or the heyday of prosperity to persuade himself that he is staunchly adhering to principle. But when pain overtakes him, when the darkness of misfortune begins to settle down upon him, and the pressure of circumstances hems him in—then he is on his trial, and has come to the testing time. In that season it will be brought to light whether he clings to self or adheres to Truth.

Principles are for our salvation in the hour of need. If we desert them in that hour, how can we be saved from the snares and pains of self?

If a man does wrong to his conscience, thinking thereby to avoid some immediate or pressing pain, he does not but increase pain and evil. The good man is less anxious to avoid pain than wrongdoing.

There is neither wisdom nor safety in deserting permanent and protective principles when our happiness seems to be at stake. If we desert the true for the pleasant, we shall lose both the pleasant and the true. But if we desert the pleasant for the true, the peace of truth will soothe away our sorrow.

If we barter the higher for the lower, emptiness and anguish will overtake us, and then, having abandoned the Eternal, where is our rock of refuge? But if we yield up the lower for the higher, the strength and satisfaction of the higher will remain with us, fullness of joy will overtake us, and we shall find in truth a rock of refuge from the evils and sorrows of life.

To find the permanent amid all the changes of life, and, having found it, adhere to it under all circumstances—this only is true happiness, this only is salvation and lasting peace.

CHAPTER-7

Light on the Sacrifice of the Self

SELF-SACRIFICE IS ONE of the fundamental principles in the teachings of the Great Spiritual Masters. It consists in yielding up self, or selfishness, so that Truth may become the source of conduct. Self is not an entity that has to be cast out, but a condition of mind that has to be converted.

The renunciation of self is not the annihilation of the intelligent being, but the annihilation of every dark and selfish desire. Self is the blind clinging to perishable things and transient pleasures as distinguished from the intelligent practice of virtue and righteousness. Self is the lusting, coveting, desiring of the heart, and it is this that must be yielded up before Truth can be known, with its abiding calm and endless peace.

To give up things will not avail; it is the lust for things that must be sacrificed. Though a man sacrifice wealth, position, friends, family, fame, home, wife, child— yea, and life also—it will avail nothing if self is not renounced.

Buddha renounced the world and all that it held dear to him, but for six years he wandered and searched and suffered and not till he yielded up the desires of the heart did he become enlightened and arrive at peace.

By giving up only the objects of self-indulgence, no peace will ensue, but torment will follow. It is self-indulgence, the desire for the object, that must be abandoned— then peace enters the heart.

Sacrifice is painful so long as there is any vestige of self remaining in the heart. While there remains in the heart a lurking desire for an unworthy object or pleasure that has been sacrificed, there will be periods of intense suffering and fierce temptation. But when the desire for the unworthy object or pleasure is put away forever from the mind, and the sacrifice is complete and perfect, then, concerning that particular object or pleasure, there can be no more suffering or temptation. So when self in its entirety is sacrificed, sacrifice, in its painful aspect, is at an end, and perfect knowledge and perfect peace are reached.

Hatred is self. Covetousness is self. Envy and jealousy are self. Vanity and boasting are self. Gluttony and sensuality are self. Lying and deception are self. Speaking evil of one's neighbor is self. Anger and revenge are self.

Self-sacrifice consists in yielding up all these dark conditions of mind and heart. The process is a painful one in its early stages, but soon a divine peace descends at intervals upon the pilgrim. Later, this peace remains longer with him, and finally, when the rays of Truth begin to be radiated in the heart, remains with him.

This sacrifice leads to peace; for in the perfect life of Truth, there is no more sacrifice, and no more pain and sorrow. For where there is no more self there is nothing to be given up. Where there is no clinging of the mind to perishable things there is nothing to be renounced. Where all has been laid on the altar of Truth, selfish love is swallowed up in divine love. And in divine love there is no thought of self, for there is the perfection of insight, enlightenment, and immortality, and therefore perfect peace.

CHAPTER-8

Light on the Management of the Mind

FOLLOWING THE LAST CHAPTER, a few hints on the management of one's mind will doubtless be opportune. Before a man can see even the necessity for thorough and complete self-government, he will have to throw off a great delusion in which so many are involved—the delusion of believing that his lapses of conduct are entirely due to those about him, and not entirely to himself.

"I could make far greater progress if I were not hindered by others," or "It is impossible for me to make any headway, seeing that I live with such irritable people," are commonly expressed complaints which spring from the error of imagining that others are responsible for one's own folly.

The violent or irritable man always blames those about him for his fits of anger, and by continually living in this delusion, he becomes more and more confirmed in his rashness and perturbations. For how can a man overcome—nay, how can he even try to overcome, his weakness if he convinces himself that it springs entirely from the actions of others? Moreover, firmly believing this as he does, he vents his anger more and more upon others in order to try to make matters better for himself, and so becomes completely lost to all knowledge of the real origin of his unhappy state.

Men cast the blame of their unprosperous acts
Upon the abettors of their own resolve,
Or anything but their weak guilty selves.

Being Responsible for Every Action

All a man's weaknesses, sins, and falls take rise in his own heart, and he alone is responsible for them. It is true there are tempters and provokers, but temptations and provocations are powerless to him who refuses to respond to them. Tempters and provokers are but foolish men, and he who gives way to them has become a willing cooperator in their folly. He is unwise and weak, and the source of troubles is in himself. The pure man cannot be tempted; the wise man cannot he provoked.

Let a man fully realize that he is absolutely responsible for his every action, and he has already gone a considerable distance along the path which leads to wisdom and peace, for he will then commence to utilize temptation as a means of growth, and the wrong conduct of others he will regard as a test of his own strength.

Socrates thanked the gods for the gift of a shrewish wife in that it enabled him the better to cultivate the virtue of patience. It is a simple and easily perceived truth that we can better grow patient by living with the impatient, better grow unselfish by living with the selfish. If a man is impatient with the impatient, he is himself impatient. If he is selfish with the selfish, then he is himself selfish. The test and measure of virtue is trial, and, like gold and precious stones, the more it is tested the brighter it shines. If a man thinks he has virtue, yet gives way when its opposing vice is presented to him, let him not delude himself—he has not yet attained to the possession of that virtue.

If a man would rise and become a man indeed, let him cease to think the weak and foolish thought, "I am hindered by others," and let him set about to discover that he is hindered only by himself. Let him realize that the giving way to another is but a revelation of his own imperfection, and lo! upon him will descend the light of wisdom, and the door of peace will open unto him, and he will soon become the conqueror of self.

The fact that a man is continually troubled and disturbed by close contact with others is an indication that he requires such contact to impel him onward to a clearer comprehension of himself; and toward a higher and more steadfast state of mind.

The very things which he regards as insurmountable hindrances will become to him the most valuable aids when he fully realizes his moral responsibility and his innate power to do right. He will then cease to blame others for his unmanly conduct, and will commence to live steadfastly under all circumstances. The scales of self-delusion will quickly fall from his eyes, and he will then see that often when he imagined himself provoked, he himself was really the provoker. As he rises above his own mental disturbances the necessity for coming in contact with the same condition in others will cease, and he will pass, by a natural process, into the company of the good and the pure. He will then awaken in others the nobility which he has arrived at in himself.

> *Be noble! and the nobleness that lies In other men, sleeping, but never dead, Will rise in majesty to meet thine own.*

CHAPTER-9

Light on Self-Control: The Door of Heaven

THE FOREMOST LESSON which the world has to learn on its way to wisdom is the lesson of self-control. All the bitter punishments which men undergo in the school of experience are inflicted because they have failed to learn this lesson. Apart from selfcontrol, salvation is a meaningless word, and peace is an impossibility. For how can a man be saved from any sin while he continues to give way to it? Or how can he realize abiding peace until he has conquered and subdued the troubles and disturbances of his mind?

Self-control is the Door of Heaven; it leads to light and peace. Without it a man is already in hell; he is lost in darkness and unrest. Men inflict upon themselves farreaching sufferings, and pass through indescribable torments, both of body and soul, through lack of self-control. Not until they resort to its practice can their sufferings and torments pass away. For it has no substitute, nothing can take its place, and there is no power in the universe that can do for a man that which he, sooner or later, must do for himself by entering the practice of self-control.

By self-control a man manifests his divine power and ascends toward divine wisdom and perfection. Every man can practice it. The weakest man can begin now, and until he does begin, his weakness will remain, or he will become weaker still.

Calling or not calling upon God or Jesus, Brahma or Buddha, Spirits or Masters, will not avail men who refuse to govern themselves and purify their hearts. Believing or disbelieving that Jesus is God, that Buddha is omniscient, or the Spirits or Masters guide human affairs, cannot help men who continue to cling to the elements of strife and ignorance and corruption within themselves.

What theological affirmation or denial can justify, or what outward power put right, the man who refuses to abandon a slanderous or abusive tongue, or give up an angry temper, or to sacrifice his impure imaginings? The flower reaches the upper light by first contending with the under darkness, and man can only reach the Light of Truth by striving against the darkness within himself.

The vast importance of self-control is not realized by men, its absolute necessity is not apprehended by them, and the spiritual freedom and glory to which it leads are hidden from their eyes. Because of this, men are enslaved and misery and suffering ensue. Let a man contemplate the violence, impurity, disease, and suffering which occur upon earth, and consider how much of it is due to want of self-control, and he will gradually come to realize the great need there is for self-control.

I say again that self-control is the Gate of Heaven, for without it neither happiness nor love nor peace can be realized and maintained. In the degree that it is lacked by a man, in just that measure will his mind and life be given over to confusion. And it is because such a large number of individuals have not yet learned to practice it that the enforced restraint of national laws is required for the maintenance of law and order and the prevention of destructive confusion.

Self-control is the beginning of virtue, and it leads to the acquisition of every noble attribute. It is the first essential quality in a well-ordered and truly religious life, and it leads to calmness, blessedness and peace. Without it, although there may be theological belief or profession, there can be no true religion, for what is religion but enlightened conduct? And what is spirituality but the triumph over the unruly tendencies of the mind?

When men both depart from and refuse to practice self-control, they fall into the great and dark delusion of separating religion from conduct. Then they persuade themselves that religion consists not in overcoming self and living blamelessly, but in holding a certain belief about Scripture, and in worshiping a certain Savior in a particular way. Hence arise the innumerable complications and confusions of letterworship, and the violence and bitter strife into which men fall in defense of their own formulated religion.

But true religion cannot be formulated; it is purity of mind, a loving heart, a soul at peace with the world. It need not be defended, for it is Being and Doing and Living. A man begins to practice religion when he begins to control himself.

CHAPTER-10

Light on Acts and Their Consequences

ONE OF THE COMMONEST EXCUSES for wrongdoing is that, if right were done, calamity would ensue. Thus the foolish concern themselves, not with the act, but with the consequence of the act, a foreknowledge of which is assumed. The desire to secure pleasant results, and to escape unpleasant consequences, is at the root of that confusion of mind which renders men incapable of distinguishing between good and evil, and prevents them from practicing the one and abandoning the other. Even when it is claimed that the wrong thing is done, not for one's self, but in order to secure the happiness of others, the delusion is the same, only it is more subtle and dangerous.

The wise concern themselves with the act, and not with its consequences. They consider, not what is pleasant or unpleasant, but what is right. Thus doing what is right only, and not straining after results, they are relieved of all burdens of doubt, desire, and fear. Nor can one who so acts ever become so involved in an extricable difficulty, or be troubled with painful perplexity. His course is so simple, straight, and plain that he can never be confused with misgivings and uncertainties.

Those who so act are said by Krishna to act "without regard to the fruits of action," and he further declares that those who have thus renounced results are supremely good, supremely wise.

Those who work for pleasant results only, and who depart from the right path when their own, or others' happiness appears to be at stake, cannot escape doubt, difficulty, perplexity, and pain. Ever forecasting probable consequences, they act in one way today, and in another way tomorrow. Unstable and blown about by the changing wind of circumstance, they become more and more bewildered, and the consequences about which they trouble do not accrue.

But they who work for righteousness only, who are careful to do the right act, putting away all selfish considerations, all thought of results, they are steadfast, unchanging, untroubled, and at peace amid all vicissitudes, and the fruits of their acts are ever sweet and blessed.

Even the knowledge, which only the righteous possess, that wrong acts can never produce good results, and that right acts can never bring about bad results, is in itself fraught with sweet assurance and peace. For whether the fruits of acts are sought or unsought, they cannot be escaped.

They who sow to self, and, ignorant of the law of Truth, think they can make their own results, reap the bitter fruits of self.

They who sow to righteousness, knowing themselves to be the reapers, and not the makers of the consequences, reap the sweet fruits of righteousness.

Right is supremely simple, and is without complexity. Error is interminably complex, and involves the mind in confusion.

To put away self and passion, and establish one's self in right-doing, this is the highest wisdom.

CHAPTER-11

Light on the Way of Wisdom

THE PATH OF WISDOM is the highest way, the way in which all doubt and uncertainty are dispelled and knowledge and surety are realized.

Amid the excitements and pleasures of the world and the surging whirlpools of human passions, Wisdom—so calm, so silent and so beautiful—is indeed difficult to find, difficult, not because of its incomprehensible complexity, but because of its unobtrusive simplicity, and because self is so blind and rash, and so jealous of its rights and pleasures.

Wisdom is "rejected of men" because it always comes right home to one's self in the form of wounding reproof, and the lower nature of man cannot bear to be reproved. Before Wisdom can be acquired, self must be wounded to the death, and because of this, because Wisdom is the enemy of self, self rises in rebellion, and will not be overcome and denied.

The foolish man is governed by his passions and personal cravings. When about to do anything he does not ask "Is this right?" but only considers how much pleasure or personal advantage he will gain by it. He does not govern his passions and act from fixed principles, but is the slave of his inclinations and follows where they lead.

The wise man governs his passions and puts away all personal cravings. He never acts from impulse and passion, but dispassionately considers what is right to be done, and does it. He is always thoughtful and self-possessed, and guides his conduct by the loftiest moral principles. He is superior to both pleasure and pain.

Wisdom cannot be found in books or travel, in learning or philosophy; it is acquired by practice only. A man may read the precepts of the greatest sages continually, but if he does not purify and govern himself he will remain foolish. A man may be intimately conversant with the writings of the greatest philosophers, but so long as he continues to give way to his passions he will not attain to wisdom.

Wisdom is right action, right doing; folly is wrong action, wrong doing. All reading, all studying is vain if man will not see his errors and give them up.

Wisdom says to the vain man, "Do not praise yourself," to the proud man, "Humble yourself," to the gossip, "Govern your tongue," to the angry man, "Subdue your anger," to the resentful man, "Forgive your enemy," to the self-indulgent man, "Be temperate," to the impure man, "Purge your heart of lust," and to all men, "Beware of small faults, do your duty faithfully, and never intermeddle with the duty of another."

These things are very simple; the doing of them is simple. But as it leads to the annihilation of self, the selfish tendencies in a man object to them and rise up in revolt against them, loving their own life of turbulent excitement and feverish pleasure, and hating the calm and beautiful silence of Wisdom. Thus men remain in folly.

Nevertheless, the Way of Wisdom is always open, is always ready to receive the tread of the pilgrim who has grown weary of the thorny and intricate ways of folly. No man is prevented from becoming wise but by himself. No man can acquire Wisdom but by his own exertions. And he who is prepared to be honest with himself, to measure the depths of his ignorance, to come face to face with his errors, to recognize and acknowledge his faults, and at once to set about the task of his own regeneration, such a man will find the way of Wisdom. Walking with humble and obedient feet, he will, in due time, come to the sweet City of Deliverance.

CHAPTER-12

Light on Disposition

"I CANNOT HELP IT, it is my disposition." How often one hears this expression as an excuse for wrongdoing. What does it imply? This, that the person who utters it believes that he has no choke in the matter, that he cannot alter his character. He believes that he must go on doing the wrong thing to the end of his days because he was "born so," or because his father or grandfather was like that; or, if not these, then someone along the family line a hundred, or two or three hundred years ago must have been afflicted, and therefore he is and must remain so. Such a belief should be uprooted, destroyed, and cast away, for it is not only without reason, it is a complete barrier to all progress, to all growth in goodness, to all development of character and noble expansion of life.

Character is not permanent; it is, indeed, one of the most changeable things in nature. If not changed by a conscious act of the will, it is being continually modified and reformed by the pressure of circumstances. Disposition is not fixed, except insofar as one fixes it by continuing to do the same thing, and by persistence in the stubborn belief that he "cannot help it." As soon as one gets rid of that belief he will find that he can help it. Further, he will find that intelligence and will are instruments which can mold disposition to any extent, and that, too, with considerable rapidity if one is in earnest.

What is disposition but a habit formed by repeating the same thing over and over again? Cease repeating (doing) the thing, and lo! the disposition is changed, the character is altered. To cease from an old habit of thought or action is, I know, difficult at first, but with each added effort the difficulty decreases, and finally disappears, and then the new and good habit is formed and the disposition is changed from bad to good, the character is ennobled, the mind is delivered from torment and is lifted into joy.

There is no need for anyone to remain the slave of a disposition which causes him unhappiness, and which he himself regards as undesirable. He can abandon it. He can break away from the slavery. He can deliver himself and be free.

CHAPTER-13

Light on Individual Liberty

WITHIN THE SPHERE of his own mind man has all power, but in the sphere of other minds and outside things, his power is limited. He can command his own mind, but he cannot command the minds of others. He can choose what he shall think, but he cannot choose what others shall think. He cannot control the weather as he wills, but he can control his mind, and decide what his mental attitude toward the weather shall be.

A man can reform the dominion of his own mind, but he cannot reform the outer world because the outer world is composed of other minds having the same freedom of choice as himself. A pure being cannot cleanse the heart of one less pure, but by his life of purity and by elucidating his experience in the attainment of purity, he can, as a teacher, act as a guide to others, and so enable them more readily and rapidly to purify themselves. But even then those others have the power to decide whether they shall accept or reject such guidance, so complete is man's choice. It is because of this dual truth—that man has no power in the realm of others' minds and yet has all power over his own mind, that he cannot avoid the consequences of his own thoughts and acts. Man is altogether powerless to alter or avert consequences, but he is altogether powerful in his choice of causative thought. Having chosen his thoughts, he must accept their full consequences. Having acted, he cannot escape the full results of his act.

Law reigns universally, and there is perfect individual liberty. A man can do as he likes, but all other men can also do as they like. A man has power to steal, but others have the power to protect themselves against the thief. Having sent out his thought, having acted his purpose, a man's power over that thought and purpose is at an end. The consequences are certain and cannot be escaped, and they will be of the nature of the thought and act which produced them—painful or blessed.

Seeing that a man can think and do as he chooses, and that all others have the like liberty, a man has to learn, sooner or later, to reckon with other minds, and until he does this he will be ceaselessly involved in suffering. To think and act apart from the consideration of others is both an abuse and an infringement of liberty. Such thoughts and acts are annulled and brought to naught by the harmonizing Principle of Liberty itself, and such annulling and bringing to naught is felt by the individual as suffering.

When the mind, rising above ignorance, recognizes the magnitude of its power within its own sphere and ceases to antagonize itself against others, it harmonizes itself to those other minds. Having acknowledged their freedom of choice, it has then realized spiritual plenitude and the cessation of suffering.

Selfishness, egotism, and despotism are, from the spiritual standpoint, transferable terms; they are one and the same thing. Every selfish thought or act is a manifestation of egotism, is an effort of despotism, and it is met with suffering and defeat. It is annulled because the Law of Liberty cannot, in the smallest particular, be annulled.

If selfishness could conquer, Liberty would be nonexistent, but selfishness fails of all results but pain, because Liberty is supreme. An act of selfishness contains two elements of egotism: namely (1) the denial of liberty of others and (2) the assertion of one's own liberty beyond its legitimate sphere. It thereby destroys itself. Despotism is death.

Man is not the creature of selfishness, he is the maker of it. It is an indication of his power—his power to disobey even the law of his being. Selfishness is power without wisdom; it is energy wrongly directed. A man is selfish because he is ignorant of his nature and power as a mental being. Such ignorance and selfishness entail suffering, and by repeated suffering and age-long experience he at last arrives at knowledge and the legitimate exercise of his power. The truly enlightened man cannot be selfish: he cannot accuse others of selfishness, or try to coerce them into being unselfish.

The selfish man is eager to bend others to his own way and will, believing it to be the only right way for all. He thereby ignorantly wastes himself in trying to check in others the power which he freely exercises himself, namely—the power to choose their own way and exercise their own will. By so doing, he places himself in direct antagonism with the like tendencies and freedom of other minds, and brings into operation the instruments of his own suffering. Hence, the ceaseless interplay of conflicting forces; the unending fires of passion; the turmoil, strife, and woe. Selfishness is misapplied power.

The unselfish man is he who, ceasing from all personal interference, abandons the "I" as the source of judgment. Having recognized his unlimited freedom through the abandonment of all egotism even in thought, he refrains from encroachment upon the boundless freedom of others. He realizes the legitimacy of their choice and their right to the free employment of their power.

However others may choose to act toward such a man, it can never cause him any trouble or suffering, because he is perfectly willing that they should so choose to act, and he harbors no wish that they should act in any other way. He realizes that his sole duty, as well as his entire power, lies in acting rightly toward them, and that he is in no way concerned with their actions toward him that is both their choice and their business. To the unselfish man, therefore, malice, envy, backbiting, jealousy, accusation, condemnation, and persecution have passed away. Having ceased to practice these things, he is not disturbed when they are hurled at him. Thus liberation from sin is liberation from suffering. The selfless man is free; he has made the servitude of sin impossible; he has broken every bond.

CHAPTER-14

Light on the Blessing and Dignity of Work

THAT "LABOR IS LIFE" is a principle pregnant with truth, and one which cannot be too often repeated or too closely studied and practiced. Labor is so often regarded as an irksome .md even degrading means of obtaining ease and pleasure, and not as what it really is—a thing happy ;md noble in itself. The lesson contained in the maxim needs to be taken to heart and more and more thoroughly learned.

Activity, both mental and physical, is the essence of life. The complete cessation of life is death, and death is immediately followed by corruption. Ease and death are closely related. The more there is of activity, the more abounding is life. The brainworker, the original thinker, the man of unceasing mental activity, is the longest-lived man in a community. The agricultural laborer, the gardener, the man of unceasing physical activity comes next with length in years.

Pure-hearted, healthy-minded people love work, and are happy in their labors. They never complain of being "overworked." It is very difficult, almost impossible, for a man to be overworked if he lives a sound and pure life. It is worry, bad habits, discontent and idleness that kill—especially idleness, for if labor is life, then idleness must be death. Let us get rid of sin before we talk about being overworked.

There are those who are afraid of work, regarding it as an enemy, and who fear a breakdown by doing too much. They have to learn what a health-bestowing friend work is. Others are ashamed of work, looking upon it as a degrading thing to be avoided. The "pure in heart and sound in head" are neither afraid nor ashamed of work, and they dignify whatsoever they undertake. No necessary work can be degrading, but if a man regards his work as such, he is already degraded, not by his task, but by his slavish vanity.

Man hath his daily work of body and mind Appointed, which declares his dignity.

The idle man who is afraid of work, and the vain man who is ashamed of it, are both on the way to poverty, if they are not already there. The industrious man, who loves work, and the man of true dignity, who glorifies work, are both on their way to affluence, if they are not already there. The lazy man is sowing the seeds of poverty and crime; the vain man is sowing the seeds of humiliation and shame. The industrious man is sowing the seeds of affluence and virtue; the dignified worker is sowing the seeds of victory and honor. Deeds are seeds, and the harvest will appear in due season.

There is a common desire to acquire riches with as little effort as possible, which is a kind of theft. To try to obtain the fruits of labor without laboring is to take the fruits of another man's labor; to try to get money without giving its equivalent is to take that which belongs to another and not one's self. What is theft but this frame of mind carried to its logical extreme?

Let us rejoice in our work. Let us rejoice that we have the strength and capacity for work, and let us increase that strength and capacity by unremitting labor.

Whatever our work may be, it is noble, and will be perceived by the world as noble, if we perform it with a noble spirit. The virtuous do not despise any labor which falls on their lot. And he who works and faints not, who is faithful, patient, and uncompromising even in the time of poverty, he will surely at last eat of the sweet fruits of his labor. Yea, even while he labors and seems to fail, happiness will be his constant companion, for, "Blessed is the man that has found his work; let him ask no other blessedness."

CHAPTER-15

Light on Good Manners and Refinement

More upward, working out the beast, And let the ape and tiger die.

ALL CULTURE IS GETTING AWAY from the beast. Evolution is a refining process, and the unwritten laws of society are inherent in the evolutionary law.

Education is intellectual culture. The scholar is engaged in purifying and perfecting his intellect; the spiritual devotee is engaged in purifying and perfecting his heart.

When a man aspires to nobler heights of achievement, and sets about the realization of his ideal, he commences to refine his nature; and the more pure a man makes himself within, the more refined, gracious, and gentle will be his outward demeanor.

Good manners have an ethical basis, and cannot be divorced from religion. To be illmannered is to be imperfect, for what are ill manners but the outward expression of inward defects? What a man does, that he is. If he acts rudely, he is a rude man; if he acts foolishly, he is a foolish man; if he acts gently, he is a gentleman. It is a mistake to suppose that a man can have a gentle and refined mind behind a rough and brutal exterior (though such a man may possess some strong animal virtues), as the outer is an expression of the inner.

One of the steps in the noble Eightfold Path to perfection as expounded by Buddha is—Right Conduct or Good Behavior. It should be plain to all that the man who has not yet learned how to conduct himself toward others in a kindly, gracious, and unselfish spirit has not yet entered the pathway of the holy life.

If a man refines his heart, he will refine his behavior; if he refines his behavior, it will help him to refine his heart.

To be coarse, brutish, and snappish may be natural to the beast, but the man who aspires to be even an endurable member of society (not to mention the higher manhood), will at once purge away any such bestial traits that may possess him.

All these things which aid in man's refinement—such as music, painting, poetry, manners—are servants and messengers of progress. Man degrades himself when he imitates the brute. Let us not mistake barbarism for simplicity or vulgarity for honesty.

Unselfishness, kindliness, and consideration for others will always be manifested outwardly as gentleness, graciousness, and refinement. To affect these graces by simulating them may seem to succeed, but it does not. Affectation and hypocrisy are soon divulged; every man's eye, sooner or later, pierces through their flimsiness, and ultimately none but the actors of them are deceived. As Emerson says:

> *"What is done for effect, is seen to be done for effect; and what is done for love, is felt to be done for love."*

Children who are well-bred are taught always to consider the happiness of others before their own: to offer others the most comfortable seat, the choicest fruit, the best tidbit, and so on, and also to do everything, even the most trivial acts, in the right way. And these two things—unselfishness and right action—are at the basis, not only of good manners, but of all ethics, religion, and true living; they represent power and skill. The selfish man is weak and unskillful in his actions. Unselfishness is the right way of thinking; good manners are the right way of acting, As Emerson, again, says:

> *"There is always a way of doing everything, if it be to boil an egg. Manners are the happy way of doing things right."*

It is a frequent error among men to imagine that the Higher Life is an ideal something quite above and apart from the common details of life, and that to neglect these or to perform them in a slovenly manner is an indication that the mind is preoccupied on "higher things." Whereas it is an indication that the mind is becoming inexact, dreamy, and weak, instead of exact, wide awake, and strong. No matter how apparently trivial the thing is which has to be done, there is a right way of doing it, and to do it in the right way saves friction, time, and trouble, conserves power, and develops grace, skill, and happiness.

The artisan has a variety of tools with which to ply his particular craft, and he is taught (and also finds by experience) that each tool must be applied to its special use, and never under any circumstances must one tool be made to do service for another. By using every tool in its proper place and in the right way, the maximum of dexterity and power is attained. Should a boy learning a trade refuse instruction, and persist in using the tools in his own way, making one tool do service for another, he would never become anything better than a clumsy bungler, and would be a failure in his trade.

It is the same throughout the whole life. If a man opens himself to receive instruction, and studies how to do everything rightly and lawfully, he becomes strong, skillful, and wise, master of himself, his thoughts and actions. But if he persists in following his momentary impulses, in doing everything as he feels prompted, not exercising thoughtfulness, and rejecting instruction, such a man will attain to nothing better than a slovenly and bungling life.

Confucius paid the strictest attention to dress, eating, deportment, passing speech—to all the so-called trivialities of life, as well as to the momentous affairs of state and the lofty moral principles which he expounded. He taught his disciples that it is the sign of a vulgar and foolish mind to regard anything as "trivial" that is necessary to be done, that the wise man pays attention to all his duties, and does everything wisely, thoughtfully, and rightly.

It is not an arbitrary edict of society that the man who persists in eating with his knife be rejected, for a knife is given to cut with, and a fork to eat with, and to put things to wrong and slovenly uses—even in the passing details of life—does not make for progress, but is retrogressive and makes for confusion.

It is not a despotic condition in the law of things that so long as a man persists in thinking and acting unkindly toward others he shall be shut out from Heaven. He shall remain in the outer pain and unrest, for selfishness is disruption and disorder. The universe is sustained by exactness, it rests on order, it demands right doing, and the searcher of wisdom will watch all his ways. He will think purely, speak gently, and act graciously, refining his entire nature, both in the letter and the spirit.

CHAPTER-16
Light on Diversities of Creeds

THOSE WHO DEPART from the common track in matters of faith, and strike out independently in search of the Higher Life, as distinguished from the letter of religious dogma, are apt to sink into a pitfall which awaits them at the first step, namely, the pitfall of pride.

Attacking "creeds" and speaking contemptuously of "the orthodox" (as though orthodoxy were synonymous with evil) are not uncommon practices among those who fondly imagine they are in possession of greater spiritual light. Departure from orthodoxy does not by any means include departure from sin. Indeed, it is frequently accompanied with increased bitterness and contempt. Change of opinion is one thing, change of heart is quite another. To withdraw one's adherence from creeds is easy; to withdraw one's self from sin is more difficult.

Hatred and pride, and not necessarily orthodoxy and conformity, are the things to be avoided. One's own sin, and not another man's creed, is the thing to be despised.

The right-minded man cannot pride himself on being "broader" than others, or assume that he is on a "higher plane" than others, or think with self-righteous contempt of those who still cling to some form of letter worship which he has abandoned.

Applying the words "narrow," "bigoted," and "selfish" to others, is not the indication of an enlightened mind. No person would wish these terms to be applied to himself, and he who is becoming truly religious does not speak of others in words which would wound him were they directed toward himself.

Those who are learning how to exercise humility and compassion are becoming truly enlightened. Thinking lowly of themselves and kindly of others; condemning their own sins with merciless logic, and thinking with tender pity of the sins of others, they develop that insight into the nature and law of things which enables them to see the truth that is in others, and in the religions of others. They do not condemn their neighbor because he holds a different faith, or because he adheres to a formal creed. Creeds must be, and he who performs faithfully his duty in his own particular creed, not interfering with or condemning his neighbor in the performance of his duty, is bringing the world nearer to perfection and peace.

Amid all the diversities of creeds there is a unifying power of undying and unalterable Love—and he or she who has Love has entered into sympathetic union with all.

He who has acquired the true spirit of Religion, who has attained to pure insight and deep charity of heart, will avoid all strife and condemnation. He will not fall into the delusion of praising his own sect (should he belong to one) and try to prove that it alone is right, or disparage other sects and try to prove that they are false. As the true man does not speak in praise of himself or his own work, so the man of humility, charity, and wisdom does not speak of his own sect as being superior to all others. He does not seek to elevate his own particular religion by picking holes in forms of faith which are held sacred by others.

Nothing more explicit and magnanimous has ever been uttered, in reference to this particular phrase of the practice of charity, than is found in the twelfth Edict of Asoka, the great Indian Ruler and Saint who lived some two or three centuries previous to the Christian era, and whose life, dedicated to the spread of Truth, testified to the beauty of his words. The edict runs thus:

> *"There should be no praising of one's own sect and decrying of other sects; but, on the contrary, a rendering of honor to other sects for whatever cause honor may be due. By so doing, both one's own sect may be helped forward, and other sects will be benefited; by acting otherwise, one's own sect will be destroyed in injuring others. Whosoever exalts his own sect by decrying others does so doubtless*

out of love for his own sect, thinking to spread abroad the fame thereof. But, on the contrary, he inflicts the more an injury upon his own sect."

These are wise and holy words; the breath of charity is in them, and they may be well pondered upon by those who are anxious to overthrow, not the religions of other men, but their own shortcomings.

It is a dark and deep-seated delusion that causes a man to think he can best advance the cause of his religion by exposing what he regards as the "evils" of other religions. The most part of it is, that while such a one rejoices in the thought that by continually belittling other sects he will perhaps at last wipe them out, and win all men to his side, he is all the time engaged in the sad work of bringing into disrepute, and thereby destroying, his own sect.

Just as every time a man slanders another, he inflicts lasting injury upon his own character and prospects, so every time one speaks evil of another sect, he soils and demeans his own. And the man who is prone to attack and condemn other religions is the one who suffers most when his own religion is attacked and condemned.

If a man does not like that his own religion should be denounced as evil and false, he should carefully guard himself that he does not condemn other religions as such. If it pleases him when his own cause is well spoken of and helped, he should speak well of and help other causes which, while differing from his own in method, have the same good view in end. In this way he will escape the errors and miseries of sectarian strife, and will perfect himself in divine charity.

The heart that has embraced gentleness and charity avoids all those blind passions which keep the fires of party strife, violence, persecution, and bitterness burning from age to age. It dwells in thoughts of pity and tenderness, scorning nothing, despising nothing, and not stirring up animosity. For he who acquires gentleness gains that clear insight into the Great Law which cannot be obtained in any other way. He sees that there is good in all sects and religions, and he makes that good his own.

Let the truth-seeker avoid divisions and offending distinctions, and let him strive after charity; for charity does not slander, backbite, or condemn. It does not think of trampling down another's, and elevating its own.

Truth cannot contradict itself. The nature of Truth is exactness, reality, undeviating certitude. Why, then, the ceaseless conflict between the religions and creeds? Is it not because of error? Contradiction and conflict belong to the domain of error, for error, being confusion, is in the nature of self-contradiction. If the Christian says, "My religion is true and Buddhism is false," and if the Buddhist says, "Christianity is false and Buddhism is true," we are confronted with an irreconcilable contradiction, for these two religions cannot be both true and false. Such a contradiction cannot come from Truth, and must therefore spring from error.

But if both these religious partisans should now say or think, "Yes, truly the contradiction springs from error, but the error is in the other man and his religion, and not me and mine," this does but intensify the contradiction. From where, then, springs the error, and where is Truth? Does not the very attitude of mind which these men adopt toward each other constitute the error? And were they to reverse that attitude, exchanging antagonism for good will, would they not perceive the Truth which does not stand in conflict with itself?

The man who says, "My religion is true, and my neighbor's is false," has not yet discovered the truth in his own religion, for when a man has done that, he will see the Truth in all religions. As behind all the universal phenomena there is but one Truth, so behind all the religions and creeds there is but one religion. For every religion contains the same ethical teaching, and all the Great Teachers taught exactly the same thing.

The precepts of the Sermon on the Mount are to be found in all religions. The life which these precepts demand was lived by all the Great Teachers and many of their disciples, for the Truth is a pure heart and a blameless life, and not a set of dogmas and opinions. All religions teach purity of heart, holiness of life, compassion, love, and good will. They teach the doing of good deeds and the giving up of selfishness and sin. These things are not dogmas, theologies, and opinions; they are things to be done, to be practiced, to be lived. Men do not differ about these things, for they are the acknowledged verities of every sect. What, then, do they differ about? About their opinions, their speculations, their theologies.

Men differ about that which is unreal, not that which is real; they fight over error, and not over Truth. The very essential of all religion (and religions) is that before a man can know anything of Truth, he must cease from fighting his fellow man, and shall learn to regard him with good will and love. How can a man do this while he is convinced that his neighbor's religion is false, and that it is his duty to do all that he can to undermine and overthrow it? This is not doing unto others as we would that they should do to us.

That which is true and real is true and real everywhere and always. There is no distinction between the pious Christian and the pious Buddhist. Purity of heart, piety of life, holy aspirations, and the love of Truth are the same in the Buddhist as the Christian. The good deeds of the Buddhist are not different from the good deeds of the Christian. Remorse for sin and sorrow for wrong thoughts and deeds springs in the hearts, not only of Christians, but of men and women of all religions. Great is the need of sympathy. Great is the need of love.

All religions are the same in that they teach the same fundamental truths. But men, instead of practicing these truths, engage opinions and speculations about things which are outside the range of knowledge and experience, and it is in defending and promulgating their own particular speculations that men become divided and engage in conflict with each other.

Condemnation is the beginning of persecution. The thought, "I am right and you are wrong," is a seed prolific of hatred. It was out of this seed that the Spanish Inquisition grew. He who would find the universal Truth must abandon egotism and quench the hateful flames of condemnation. He must remove from his heart the baneful thought, "All others are wrong," and think the illuminating thought, "It is I who am wrong." And having thus thought, he will cease from sin, and will live in love and good will toward all, making no distinctions, engaging in no divisions, a peacemaker and not a partisan. Thus living charitably disposed to all, he will become one with all. He will comprehend the Universal Truth, the Eternal Religion; for while error and selfishness divide, Truth demonstrates Truth and Religion unifies.

CHAPTER-17

Light on Law and Miracle

THE LOVE OF THE WONDERFUL is an element in human nature which, like passions and desires, requires to be curbed, directed, and finally transmuted; otherwise superstition and the obscuration of reason and insight cannot be avoided. The idea of a miracle must be transcended before the orderly, eternal, and beneficent nature of the law can be perceived. Then peace and certainty, which a knowledge of kw bestows, can be enjoyed.

Just as a child when its eyes are opened to the phenomena of this world becomes involved in wonder, and revels in tales of giants and fairies, so when a man first opens his mental eyes to spiritual things does he become involved in stories of marvels and miracles. As a child at last becomes a man and leaves behind the crudities of childhood, understanding more accurately the relative nature of the phenomena around him, so with a fuller spiritual development and greater familiarity with the inner realities a man at last leaves behind the era of childish wonderment. He comes into touch with the law of things, and governs his life by principles that are fixed and invariable.

Law is universal and eternal, and, although vast areas of knowledge are waiting to be revealed, cause and effect will ever prevail. Every new discovery, every truth revealed, will serve to bring one nearer to a realization of the beauty, stability, and supremacy of the law. And very gladdening it is to know that law is inviolable and eternal throughout every department of nature, For then we know that the same operations of the universe are ever the same, and can therefore be discovered, understood, obeyed. This is a ground of certainty, and therefore of great hope and joy. The idea of miracle is a denial of law and the substitution of an arbitrary and capricious power.

It is true that around the lives of the Great Teachers of humanity stories of miracles have grown, but they have emanated from the undeveloped minds of the people, not from the Teachers themselves.

Lao-Tze expounded the Supreme Law, or Reason, which admits no miracle, yet his religion has today become so corrupted with the introduction of the marvelous as to be little better than a mass of superstition.

Even Buddhism, whose founder declared that, "Seeing that the Law of Karma (cause and effect) governs all things, the disciple who aims at performing miracles does not understand the doctrine," and that, "The desire to perform miracles arises either from covetousness or vanity," has surrounded, in its corrupted form, the life of its Great Master with a number of miracles.

Even during the lifetime of Ramakrishna, the Hindu teacher who died in 1886, and who is regarded by his disciples as an incarnation of Deity to this age, all sorts of miracles were attributed to him by the people, and are now associated with his name. Yet, according to Max Muller, these miracles are without any foundation of evidence or fact, and Ramakrishna himself ridiculed and repudiated miracle.

As men become more enlightened, miracles and wonder-working will be expunged from religion, and the orderly beauty of Law and the ethical grandeur of obedience to the Law will become revealed and known. No man who desires to perform miracles or astral or psychological wonders, who is curious to see invisible or supernatural beings, or who is ambitious to become a "Master" or an "Adept," can attain a clear perception of Truth and the living of the highest life. Childish wonderment about things must be supplanted by knowledge of things, and vanity is a complete barrier to the entrance of the true path which demands of the disciple lowliness of heart, humility. He is on the true path who is cultivating kindness, forbearance, and a loving heart. The marks of a true Master are not miracles and wonder-working, but infinite patience, boundless compassion, spotless purity, and a heart at peace with all.

CHAPTER-18

Light on War and Peace

WAR SPRINGS FROM INWARD STRIFE. "War in heaven" precedes war on earth. When the inward spiritual harmony is destroyed by division and conflict, it will manifest itself outwardly in the form of war. Without this inward conflict war could not be, nor can war cease until the inward harmony is restored.

War consists of aggression and resistance, and after the fight has commenced both combatants are like aggressors and resisters. Thus the effort to put an end to war by aggressive means produces war.

"I have set myself stubbornly against the war spirit," said a man a short time ago. He did not know that he was, by that attitude of mind, practicing and fostering the war spirit.

To fight against war is to produce war. It is impossible to fight for peace, because all fighting is the annihilation of peace. To think of putting an end to war by denouncing and fighting it is the same as to try to quench fire by throwing straw upon it.

He, therefore, who is truly a person of peace, does not resist war, but practices peace. He, therefore, who takes sides and practices attack and defense is responsible for war, for he is always at war in his mind. He cannot know the nature of peace, for he has not arrived at peace in his own heart.

The true man of peace is he who has put away from his mind the spirit of quarreling and party strife, who neither attacks others nor defends himself, and whose heart is at peace with all. Such a man has already laid in his heart the foundations of the empire of peace; he is a peacemaker, for he is at peace with the whole world and practices the spirit of peace under all circumstances.

Very beautiful is the spirit of peace, and it says, "Come and rest." Bickerings, quarreling, party divisions—these must be forever abandoned by him who would establish peace.

War will continue so long as men will allow themselves, individually, to be dominated by passion, and only when men have quelled the inward tumult will the outward horror pass away.

Self is the great enemy, the producer of all strife, and the maker of many sorrows. He, therefore, who will bring about peace on earth, let him overcome egotism, let him subdue his passions, let him conquer himself.

CHAPTER-19

Light on the Brotherhood of Man

THERE IS NO LACK OF WRITING and preaching about "universal brotherhood," and it has been adopted as a leading article of faith by many newly formed societies. But what is so urgently needed to begin with is not universal brotherhood, but particular Brotherhood. That is, the adoption of a magnanimous, charitable, and kindly spirit toward those with whom we come in immediate contact; toward those who contradict, oppose and attack us, as well as toward those who love and agree with us.

I make a very simple statement of truth when I say that until such particular brotherhood is practiced, universal brotherhood will remain a meaningless term. For universal brotherhood is an end, a goal, and the way to it is by particular brotherhood. The one is sublime and far-reaching consummation, the other is the means by which that consummation must be realized.

I remember on one occasion reading a paper devoted largely to the teachings of universal brotherhood, and the leading article—a long and learned one— was an exposition of this subject. But on turning over a few more pages, I found another piece by the same writer in which he accused of misrepresentation, lying, and selfishness, not his enemies, but the brethren of his own Society, who bear, at least as far as such sins are concerned, stainless reputations.

A scriptural writer asked the question, "If a man does not love his brother whom he has seen, how can he love God whom he has not seen?" In the same manner, if a man does not love the brother whom he knows, how can he love people of all creeds and all nations whom he does not know?

To write articles on universal brotherhood is one thing; to live in peace with one's relations and neighbors and to return good for evil is quite another.

To endeavor to propagate universal brotherhood while fostering in our heart some sparks of envy, spite, and resentment, malice, or hatred, is to be self-deluded; for thus shall we be all the time hindering and denying, by our actions, that which we eulogize by our words. So subtle is such self-delusion, that, until the very heights of love and wisdom are reached, we are all liable at any moment to fall into it.

It is not because our fellow men do not hold our views, or follow our religion, or see as we see that universal brotherhood remains unrealized, but because of the prevalence of ill will. If we hate, avoid, and condemn others because they differ from us, all that we may say or do in the cause of universal brotherhood will be another snare to our feet, a mockery to our aspirations, and a farce to the world at large.

Let us, then, remove all hatred and malice from our hearts. Let us be filled with goodwill toward those who try and test us by their immediate nearness. Let us love them that hate us, and think magnanimously of those who condemn us or our doctrine—in a word, let us take the first step toward universal brotherhood, by practicing brotherhood in the place where it is most needed. And as we succeed in being brotherly in these important particulars, universal brotherhood will be found to be not far distant.

CHAPTER-20

Light on Life's Sorrows

THERE IS GREAT SORROW IN THE WORLD. This is one of the supreme facts of life. Grief and affliction visit every heart, and many that are today reveling in hilarious joy or sinful riot, will tomorrow be smitten low with sorrow. Suddenly, and with swift and silent certainty, comes its poignant arrow, entering the human heart, slaying its joy, laying low its hopes, and shattering all its earthly plans and prospects. Then the humbled, smitten soul reflects, and enters deeply and sympathetically into the hidden meanings of human life.

In the dark times of sorrow, men and women approach very near to Truth. When in one brief hour the built up hopes of many years of toil fall like a toy palace, and all earthly pleasures burst and vanish like petty bubbles in the grasp, then the crushed spirit, bewildered, tempest-tossed, and without a refuge, gropes in dumb anguish for the Eternal, and seeks its abiding peace.

"Blessed are they that mourn," said the Teacher of the West, and the Teacher of the East declared that, "Where there is great suffering there is great bliss." Both of these sayings express the truth that sorrow is a teacher and purifier. Sorrow is not the end of life— though it is, in its consummation, the end of the worldly life—it leads the bewildered spirit into rest and safety; for the end of sorrow is joy and peace.

Strong searcher for Truth! Strenuous fighter against self and passion! Seasons of sorrow must be your portion for a time. While any vestige of self remains, temptations will assail you; the veil of illusion will cloud your spiritual vision, producing sorrow and unrest. When heavy clouds settle down upon your spirit, accept the darkness as your own, and pass through it bravely into the cloudless light beyond. Bear well in mind t hat nothing can overtake you that does not belong to you and that is not for your eternal good. As the poet has truly sung—

Nor space nor time, nor deep nor high Can keep my own away from me.

And not alone are the bright things of life yours; the dark things are yours also.

When difficulties and troubles gather thickly about you; when failures come and friends fall away; when the tongue that has sweetly praised you, bitterly blames; when beloved lips that pressed against your lips, the soft, warm kisses of love, taunt and mock you in the lonely hour of your solitary grief; or when you lay beneath the sod the cold casket of clay that but yesterday held the responsive spirit of your beloved—when these things overtake you, remember that the hour of your Gethsemane has come. The cup of anguish is yours to drink. Drink it silently and murmur not, for in that hour of oppressive darkness and blinding pain no prayer will save you, no cry to heaven will bring you sweet relief. Faith and patience only will give you the strength to endure, and to go through your crucifixion with a meek and gentle spirit, not complaining, blaming no one, but accepting it as your own.

When one has reached the lowest point of sorrow; when, weak and exhausted, and overcome with a sense of powerlessness, he cries to God for help, and there comes no answering comfort and no relief—then, discovering the painfulness of sorrow and the insufficiency of prayer alone, he is ready to enter the path of self-renunciation, ready to purify his heart, ready to practice self-control, ready to become a spiritual athlete, and to develop that divine and invincible strength which is born of self-mastery.

He will find the cause of sorrow in his own heart, and will remove it. He will learn to stand alone; not craving sympathy from any, but giving it to all. Not thoughtlessly sinning and remorsefully repenting, but studying how not to commit sin. Humbled by innumerable defeats, and chastened by many sufferings, he will learn how to act blamelessly toward others, how to be gentle and strong, kind and steadfast, compassionate and wise.

Thus he will gradually rise above sorrow, and at last Truth will dawn upon his mind, and he will understand the meaning of abiding peace. His mental eye will be open to perceive the Cosmic Order. He will be blessed with the Vision of the Law, and will receive the Beatific Bliss.

When the true order of things is perceived, sorrow is transcended. When the contracted personal self, which hugs its own fleeting pleasures and broods over its own petty disappointments and dissatisfactions, is broken up and cast away, then the larger life of Truth enters the mind, bringing bliss and peace; and the Universal Will takes the place of self. The individual becomes one with humanity. He forgets self in his love for all. His sorrow is swallowed up in the bliss of Truth.

Thus when you have, by experience, entered completely into the sorrow that is never lifted from the heart of humankind; when you have reaped and eaten all the bitter fruits of your own wrong thoughts and deeds—then divine compassion for all suffering beings will be born in your heart, healing all your wounds and drying all your tears. You will rise again into a new and heavenly life, where the sting of sorrow cannot enter, for there is no self there. After the crucifixion comes the transfiguration; the sorrowless state is reached through sorrow, and "the wise do not grieve."

Ever remember this—in the midst of sin and sorrow there abides the world of Truth. Redemption is at hand. The troubled may find peace; the impure may find purity. Healing awaits the broken-hearted. The weak will be adorned with strength, and the downtrodden will be lifted up and glorified.

CHAPTER-21

Light on Life's Changes

THE TENDENCY OF THINGS to advance from a lower to a higher level, and from high to higher still, is universal. The worlds exist in order that beings may experience, and by experiencing, acquire knowledge and increase in wisdom.

Evolution is only another name for progress. It signifies perpetual change, but a purposeful change, a change accompanied by growth. Evolution does not mean the creation of a new being from a being of a different order. It means the modification of beings by experience and change; and such modification is progress.

The fact of change is ever before us. Nothing can escape it. Plants, animals, and human beings germinate, reach maturity, and pass into decay. Even the lordly suns and their attendant worlds rolling through illimitable spaces, although their life is reckoned in millions of years, at last decay and perish after having passed through innumerable changes. We cannot say of any being or object—"This will remain forever as it is," for even while we are saying it, the being or object would be undergoing change.

Sadness and suffering accompany this change; and beings mourn for that which has departed, for the things which are lost and gone. Yet in reality change is good, for it is the open door to all achievement, advancement, and perfection.

Mind, as well as matter, is subject to the same change. Every experience, every thought, every deed, changes a person. There is little resemblance between the elderly and their period of childhood and youth.

An eternally fixed, unchangeable being is not known. Such a being may be assumed, but it is a postulate only. It is not within the range of human observation and knowledge. A being not subject to change would be a being outside progress.

There is a teaching which declares that man has a spiritual soul that is eternally pure, eternally unchanged, eternally perfect, and that sinning, suffering, changing man as we see him is an illusion—that, indeed, the spiritual soul is the man, and the other is unreality.

There is another teaching that affirms that man is eternally imperfect, that stainless purity can never be reached, and that perfection is an impossibility, an illusion.

It will be found that these two extremes have no relation to human experience. They are both of the nature of speculative metaphysics which stand in opposition to the facts of life; so much so that the adherents of these two extremes deny the existence of the commonest everyday facts of human experience. That which is assumed is regarded as real; the facts of life are declared to be unreal.

It is well to avoid both these extremes, and find the middle way of human experience. It is well to avoid opinions and speculations of our own or others, it is well to refer to the facts of life. We see that man passes through birth and growth and old age, that he experiences sin, sickness, and death; that he sorrows and suffers, aspires and rejoices; and that he is ever looking forward to greater purity and striving toward perfection. These are not opinions, speculations, or metaphysics—they are universal facts.

If man were already perfect, there would be no need for him to be perfected, and all moral teaching would be useless and ridiculous. Moreover, a perfect being could not be subject to illusion and unreality.

On the other hand, if a man could never attain to purity and perfection, his aspirations and striving would be useless. They would indeed be mockeries; and the heavenly perfection of saintly and divine men and women would have to be belittled and denied.

We see around us sin, sorrow, and suffering; and we see before us, in the lives of the great teachers, the sinless, sorrowless, divine state. Therefore, we know that man is an imperfect being, yet capable of, and destined for, perfection. The divine state toward which he aspires, he will reach. The fact that he so ardently desires it means that he can reach it, even if the fact were not demonstrated in those great ones who have already attained.

Man is not a compound of two beings, one real and perfect, the other unreal and imperfect. He is one and real, and his experiences are real. His imperfection is apparent, and his advancement and progress are also apparent.

The realities of life claim men in spite of their metaphysics, and all come under the same law of change and progress. He who affirms the eternal sinlessness and perfection of man, should not, to be logical and consistent, ever speak of sins and faults, of disease and death; yet he refers to these things as matters to be dealt with. Thus in theory he denies the existence of that which he habitually recognizes in practice.

He also who denies the possibility of perfection should not aspire or strive; yet we find him practicing self-denial and striving ceaselessly toward perfection.

Holding to the theoretical does not absolve one from the inevitable. The teacher of the unreality of sickness, old age, and death is at last caught in the toils of disease, succumbs to age, and disappears in death.

Change is not only inevitable; it is the constant and unvarying law. Without it, everything would remain forever as it is, and there would be neither growth nor progress.

The strenuous struggle of all life is a prophecy of its perfection. The looking upward of all beings is evidence of their ceaseless ascension. Aspirations, ideals, moral aims, while they denote mans imperfection, assuredly point to his future perfection. They are neither unnecessary nor aimless, but are woven into the fabric of things. They belong to the vital essence of the universe.

Whatsoever a man believes or disbelieves, what theories he holds or does not hold, one thing is certain—he is found in the stream of life, and must think and act. To think and act is to experience; and to experience is to change and develop.

That man is conscious of sin means that he can become pure; that he abhors evil signifies that he can reach up to Good; that he is a pilgrim in the land of error assures us, without doubt, that he will at last come to the beautiful city of Truth.

CHAPTER-22

Light on the Truth of Transitoriness

IT IS WELL SOMETIMES to meditate deeply and seriously on the truth of Transitoriness. By meditation we will come to perceive how all compounded things must pass away; yea, how even while they remain they are already in the process of passing away. Such meditation will soften the heart, deepen the understanding, and render one more fully conscious of the sacred nature of life.

What is there that does not pass away, among all the things of which a man says, "This will be mine tomorrow"? Even the mind is continually changing. Old characteristics die and pass away, and new ones are formed. In the midst of life all things are dying. Nothing endures; nothing can be retained. Things appear and then disappear; they become, and then they pass away.

The ancient sages declared the visible universe to be Maya, illusion, meaning thereby that impermanency is the antithesis of Reality. Change and decay are in the very nature of visible things, and they are unreal—illusory—in the sense that they pass away forever.

He who would ascend into the realm of Reality, who would penetrate into the world of Truth, must first perceive, with no uncertain vision, the transitory nature of the things of life. He must cease to delude himself into believing that he can retain his hold on his possessions, his body, his pleasures and objects of pleasure. For as the flower fades and as the leaves of the tree fall and wither, so must these things, in their season, pass away forever.

The perception of the Truth of Transitoriness is one of the few great steps in wisdom, for when it is fully grasped, and its lesson has sunk deeply into the heart, the clinging to perishable things which is the cause of all sorrow, will be yielded up, and the search for the Truth which abides will be accelerated.

Anguish is rife because men and women set their hearts on the acquisition of things that perish, because they lust for the possession of those things which even when obtained cannot be retained.

There is no sorrow that would not vanish if the clinging to transient things were given up. There is no grief that would not be dispersed if the desire to have and to hold things which in their very nature cannot endure were taken out of the heart.

Tens of thousands of grief-stricken hearts are today bewailing the loss of some loved object which they called theirs in days that are past, are weeping over that which is gone forever and cannot be restored.

Men are slow to learn the lessons of experience and to acquire wisdom, and unnumbered griefs and pains and sorrows have failed to impress them with the Truth of Transitoriness. He who clings to that which is impermanent cannot escape sorrow, and the intensity of his sorrow will be measured by the strength of his clinging. He who sets his heart on perishable things embraces the companionship of grief and lamentation.

Men and women cannot find wisdom because they will not renounce the clinging to things. They believe that clinging to perishable objects is the source of happiness, and not the cause of sorrow. They cannot escape unrest and enter into the life of peace because desire is difficult to quench, and the immediate and transitory pleasure which gratified desire affords is mistaken for abiding joy.

It is because the true order of things is not understood that grief is universal. It is ignorance of the fleeting nature of things that lies at the root of sorrow.

The sting of anguish will be taken out of life when the lust to hold and to preserve the things of decay is taken out of the heart.

Sorrow is ended for him who sees things as they are; who, realizing the nature of transiency, detaches his heart and mind from the things that perish.

There is a right use for perishable things, and when they are rightly used, and not doted upon for themselves alone, their loss will cause no sorrow.

If a rich man thinks in his heart, "My riches and possessions are no part of me, nor can I call them mine, seeing that when I am summoned to depart from this world, I cannot take them with me; they are entrusted to me to be used rightly, and I mil employ them to the best of my ability for the good of men and for the world," such a man, though surrounded by luxuries and responsibilities, will be lifted above sorrow, and will draw near to the Truth. On the other hand, if the poor man does not covet riches and possessions, his condition will cause him no anxiety and unrest.

He who by a right understanding of life rids his heart of all selfish grasping and clinging, who uses things wisely and in their proper place, and who, with chastened heart, and mind clarified of all thirsty desires, remains serene and self-contained in the midst of all changes, such a man will find Truth. He will stand face to face with Reality.

For in the midst of all error there abides the Truth; at the heart of the transiency there reposes the Permanent; and illusion does but veil the eternal and unchanging Reality.

The nature of that Reality it is not my purpose to deal with here. Let it suffice that I indicate that it is only found by abandoning, in the heart, all that is not of Love and Compassion, Wisdom and Purity. In these things there is no element of transitoriness, no sorrow, and no unrest.

When the truth of Transitoriness is well perceived, and when the lesson contained in the truth of Transitoriness is well learned, then does a man set out to find the abiding Truth; then does he wean his heart from those selfish elements which are productive of sorrow.

He whose treasure is Truth, who fashions his life in accordance with Wisdom, will find the Joy which does not pass away. He will leave behind him the land of lamentation, and, crossing the wide ocean of illusion, will come to the Sorrowless Shore.

CHAPTER-23

The Light That Never Goes Out

AMID THE MULTITUDE of conflicting opinions and theories, and caught in the struggle of existence, whither shall the confused truth-seeker turn to find the path that leads to peace unending? To what refuge shall he fly from the uncertainties and sorrows of change?

Will he find peace in pleasure? Pleasure has its place, and in its place it is good; but as an end, as a refuge, it affords no shelter. He who seeks it as such does but increase the anguish of life; for what is more fleeting than pleasure, and what is more empty than the heart that seeks satisfaction in so ephemeral a thing? There is, therefore, no abiding refuge in pleasure.

Will he find peace in wealth and worldly success?

Wealth and worldly success have their place, but they are fickle and uncertain possessions, and he who seeks them for themselves alone will be burdened with many anxieties and cares. When the storms of adversity sweep over his glittering yet frail habitation, he will find himself helpless and exposed. But even should he maintain such possessions throughout life, what satisfaction will they afford him in the hour of death? There is no abiding refuge in wealth and worldly success.

Will he find peace in health? Health has its place, and it should not be thrown away or despised, but it belongs to the body which is destined for dissolution, and is therefore perishable. Even should health be maintained for a hundred years, the time will come when the physical energies will decline and debility and decay will overtake them. There is no abiding refuge in health.

Will he find refuge in those whom he dearly loves? Those whom he loves have their place in his life. They afford him means of practicing unselfishness, and thereby arriving at Truth. He should cherish them with loving care, and consider their needs before his own. But the time will come when they will be separated from him, and he will be left alone.

There is no abiding refuge in loved ones.

Will he find peace in this Scripture or that? Scripture fills an important place. As a guide it is good, but it cannot be a refuge, for one may know the Scripture by heart, and yet be in sore conflict and unrest. The theories of men are subject to successive changes, and no limit can be set to the variety of textual interpretations. There is no abiding refuge in Scripture.

Will he find rest in this teacher or that? The teacher has his place, and as an instructor he renders good service. But teachers are numerous, and their differences are many. Though one may regard his particular teacher as in possession of the Truth, that teacher will one day be taken from him. There is no abiding refuge in a teacher.

Will he find peace in solitude? Solitude is good and necessary in its place, but he who courts it as a lasting refuge will be like one perishing of thirst in a waterless desert. He will escape men and the turmoil of the city, but he will not escape himself and the unrest of the heart. There is no abiding rest in solitude.

If, then, the seeker can find no refuge in pleasure, in success, in health, in family and friends, in Scripture, in the teacher, or in solitude, whither shall he turn to find that sanctuary which shall afford abiding peace?

Let him take refuge in righteousness. Let him fly to the sanctuary of a purified heart. Let him enter the pathway of a blameless, stainless life, and walk it meekly and patiently until it brings him to the eternal temple of Truth in his own heart.

He who has taken refuge in Truth, even in the habitation of a wise understanding and a loving and steadfast heart, is the same whether in pleasure or pain; wealth or poverty; success or failure; health or sickness; with friends or without; in solitude or noisy haunts; and he is independent of bibles and teachers, for the spirit of Truth instructs him. He perceives without fear or sorrow the change and decay which are in all things. He has found peace; he has entered the abiding sanctuary; he knows the Light that will never go out.

* * *

www.ingramcontent.com/pod-product-compliance
Lightning Source LLC
La Vergne TN
LVHW090936230826
846093LV00006BA/203

* 9 7 8 9 3 5 4 6 2 5 3 3 6 *